EFFECTIVE EMPLOYEE PARTICIPATION

EFFECTIVE EMPLOYEE PARTICIPATION

A Practical Guide to Value Management

Lynn Tylczak

KOGAN
PAGE

First published in the United States of America in 1990 by Crisp Publications Inc, 95 First Street, Los Altos, California 94022, USA.

This edition first published in Great Britain in 1990 by Kogan Page Ltd, 120 Pentonville Road, London N1 9JN

British Library Cataloguing in Publication Data

A CIP record for this book is available from the British Library.

ISBN 0-7494-0285-7
ISBN 0-7494-0286-5 Pbk

Typeset by the Castlefield Press, Wellingborough, Northants.
Printed and bound in Great Britain by
Biddles Limited, Guildford.

Contents

Preface

Managers who want to purchase the best in goods and services must watch their expenditure. Since seeing is believing, they may be blinded to all but the most visible business ratio: return on investment (ROI).

However, day-to-day ROI figures are rarely of importance in the long run. They are too restricted for the far-sighted manager. Consider training costs or research and development expenditures. Both are current expenses that may not affect the assets column of the balance sheet for months to come, whereas the concept that offers managers their greatest profit payback is ingenuity. It requires the proper work environment, a strong employee suggestion scheme, employee training and assistance, and a positive attitude.

This book will help you to create all four. You will learn:

- The power of employee suggestions

- How to create an environment that encourages creativity

- A step-by-step process that employees can use to identify, analyse and refine profitable ideas

- How to turn apathetic automatons into full participators.

Lynn Tylczak

Acknowledgements

Thanks are due to all the people who helped with the research for this book – particularly John Maurer, Gary Robinson, Thomas R Chamberlain and Pete Megani.

About This Book

This book is two for the price of one. It tells you about successful suggestion schemes and about Value Management (VM) – a double promise of success for the businessperson who puts its guidelines into practice.

Chapter 1 shows how involving employees in Value Management can, or rather will, save money while improving quality, productivity and morale. VM is working for more than half those companies who search for excellence. It will work for yours.

Chapter 2 looks at the requirements for a successful employee suggestion scheme. Are you doing everything necessary to make your scheme successful? Remember money isn't everything. Many successful suggestion schemes could be financed out of petty cash!

Chapter 3 introduces VM – a little-known technique used by top companies to help employees find new ways of achieving more (quality, productivity, service) at less cost. These Value Management methods can be applied by virtually any employee to virtually any problem with a virtual guarantee of success.

Chapter 4 is Value Management in action, a real-life case study of how VM helped a typist to increase her department's productivity on one business form by over 800 per cent.

Any company can increase quality while cutting costs, because any company can implement Value Management (the method) and a successful suggestion scheme (the vehicle). Thanks to the information in this book, you're only a short read away!

CHAPTER 1
What's in it for Me?

The power of suggestions

In the late 1800s, Lister & Co was Britain's leading silk supplier. Its incredible profits set the standard for corporate fashion and over-indulgence. One mill was so large that a car could have been driven round the top of its chimney.

In 1912 a Lister employee, scientist/chemist Samuel Courtauld, showed management a new synthetic silk he had created. He called it 'rayon.' Lister management tore the ragamuffin's idea to shreds, saying that the public would insist on real silk. So poor Samuel Courtauld had to set out on his own to create – and profit from – a multi-million pound industry.

Can a good employee suggestion scheme really turn an innovative sow's ear into a silk purse – one that will keep paying dividends far into the future? There are no guarantees, but there are some certainties. In the next few pages, you will see what a well-designed and well-administered employee suggestion scheme can do for you. It offers perceptive front-line managers the opportunity to move their departments ahead on all fronts.

Desired changes

If you are not totally convinced about the idea of upgrading your employee suggestion scheme, consider the benefits it will bring. Set aside a few minutes. List all the areas in your business that you would like to improve. Think in broad terms:

people, products, profits, procedures, processes, and anything else.

I would like to improve:

_____

_____

_____

_____

_____

_____

_____

_____

_____

_____

Transpired changes

Match your desired changes to the 'transpired changes' listed below. The chances are that the list includes all your desired changes plus a few other ideas you wish you'd listed. These transpired changes are improvements documented by top international companies (Honeywell, IBM and Westinghouse, to name but a few) as a result of internal Value Management employee suggestion schemes.

Transpired changes:

- *Cost improvements and other money matters.* Substantial cost savings, improved cash flow, elimination of unnecessary or costly items.

- *Quality corrections.* Higher quality products or services, better quality control.

- *Progress in products or services.* Substantial improvements in product competitiveness, performance, reliability, packaging and weight.

- *Improved procedures or processes.* Streamlined internal logistics, shorter production lead time, improved availability of parts.

- *Personnel benefits.* Increased leadership qualities, better framework, improved communications, higher productivity, more workforce creativity, greater acceptance and use of new ideas and technology, higher morale, lower rate of turnover.

The value of employee input

Concentrating on changes instigated by employees rather than managers offers another range of benefits:

- Employees often have a better 'feel' than managers for how procedures and processes could be improved. Familiarity with the job does not breed contempt: it breeds creativity ('How would I do this if it were up to me? How could I make my job easier?'). Hands-on experience creates an awareness of opportunities and problems that is not always shared by 'hands-off' managers.

- Employees may have a more diverse background than managers. Workers employed by the hour are more transient than managers. Ideas picked up on other jobs can often shed light on problem areas ('Where I used to work we solved that by . . .' 'We used to . . . ').

- Employees can experiment without upsetting the applecart. They can tinker with new ideas and generate very little attention. Managers investigating the same procedure would create concern.

- Employee-based ideas fare better in the unfair game of politics. Which ideas get a better reception from the workforce: proposals from peers or management-initiated manifestos?

- Employee suggestion schemes improve the way the organisation works. You can't do all the work yourself: you have to delegate. A sound employee suggestion scheme will facilitate – rather than hinder – your efforts.

CHAPTER 2

Components of a Successful Suggestion Scheme

The three components

Like a three-legged stool, a successful employee suggestion scheme has three important 'support systems.' Schemes without these basic components – Visibility, Ego-boosters, and Structure – are unlikely to succeed.

Building a profitable scheme is relatively easy. The 50 strategies that follow are a good place to start. For each item, ask yourself:

- Does our company use this tactic?

- If not, why not? Is it appropriate for us?

- Could we adapt it to fit our specific needs and circumstances?

- Do I have the authority to implement it? If not, who does?

- When could we start doing this?

- Who would handle any related administrative tasks?

Component 1: visibility

The value of visibility is obvious – what is out of sight is also out of mind. Here are a few tactics to help employees keep their eyes open for potential benefits and their minds on innovative improvements.

	Within my authority	Needs additional authority	When can we start?
1. Reward suggestions with framed certificates.			
2. Post accepted suggestions on the office notice-board.			
3. Post accepted suggestions in reception.			
4. Put up employees' photos with their suggestions (people often know faces, but not names).			
5. Distribute congratulatory leaflets.			
6. Reward the best suggestion with a trophy.			
7. Let participants use a specially designated parking space.			
8. Acknowledge suggestions on an external notice-board.			

	Within my authority	Needs additional authority	When can we start?
9. Acknowledge suggestions over the PA system.			
10. Acknowledge suggestions at regular meetings.			
11. Congratulate the employee personally and publicly.			
12. Acknowledge past suggestions in speeches, memos, training seminars.			
13. Send a press release about significant suggestions to the local newspaper.			
14. Send a press release about important suggestions to appropriate trade journals or suppliers.			
15. Write an article about significant suggestions and print it in your firm's newsletter (even better, get it included in the company's quarterly report).			
16. Use the staff member and his or her suggestion in company advertising.			

Component 2: ego-boosters

There's an old saying: 'You attract more flies with honey than with vinegar.' The same holds true for your employee suggestion scheme. If a worker's experience with your scheme leaves him or her feeling buoyant, that worker will come back for more.

These personal benefits will help you to reward employees (not necessarily financially!) for a job well done.

	Within my authority	Needs additional authority	When can we start?
17. Write a personal letter to the employee thanking him or her for the suggestion.			
18. Write a personal letter to his or her family, recognising the employee's contribution.			
19. Write a letter to your boss, acknowledging the employee's success.			
20. Write a letter for the employee's personnel records, acknowledging his or her idea (particularly important to promotion-conscious people).			
21. Ask the head of the organisation to write a letter of congratulation.			

	Within my authority	Needs additional authority	When can we start?
22. Write a 'thank you' note to the employee on personal – not company – stationery.			
23. Express personal admiration.			
24. Voice your appreciation on a continuing basis.			
25. Mention the worker's contribution at his or her regular assessment interviews.			
26. Consider – but don't feel bound to offer – financial rewards.			

Component 3: structure

The only way to avoid chaos is to institute a plan. Here are a few helpful hints.

	Within my authority	Needs additional authority	When can we start?
27. Ensure that the scheme is sensitive to people's feelings, values and needs.			

	Within my authority	Needs additional authority	When can we start?
28. Make sure that the structure is understood. Keep the structure of the scheme as simple as possible.			
29. Help employees to generate ideas (for example, suggest areas for improvement, demonstrate how past ideas can be adapted to newer needs).			
30. Help with any necessary research.			
31. Train employees to spot potential improvements.			
32. Encourage team efforts and suggestions.			
33. Facilitate interdepartmental brainstorming.			
34. Make any forms easy to use.			
35. Develop easily understood procedures and rules.			

	Within my authority	Needs additional authority	When can we start?
36. Make the scheme easy to implement physically (readily available forms, boxes for completed forms).			
37. Use self-duplicating forms.			
38. Use professional-looking forms that employees will take seriously.			
39. Number the suggestion forms to emphasise their importance.			
40. Set up a formal and ongoing suggestions committee.			
41. Make sure that each suggestion has a designated supporter on the committee.			
42. Make sure that each suggestion gets a formal and fair hearing.			
43. Keep employees informed about the progress of their idea(s).			
44. Set deadlines for committee decisions.			

	Within my authority	Needs additional authority	When can we start?
45. Make sure that employees are told why their idea was, or was not, accepted.			
46. Allow employees to adapt suggestions when appropriate.			
47. Make sure that internal promotion forms include a space to note scheme participation.			
48. Make sure that employee assessment forms include a space to note scheme participation.			
49. Keep a company scrapbook and regularly paste in employee suggestions.			
50. **Demonstrate serious and ongoing top management support**			

Selling the support systems

Visibility, ego-boosters and structure will sell a suggestion scheme to your workers. Convincing other managers to take up the scheme requires an entirely different approach. The key to success is this: managers are not interested in how a scheme *works*, they are far more interested in *what it can do*. For example:

The benefits of visibility:
- A positive corporate image (we encourage innovation)

- More concentration on quality and cost goals

- Positive reinforcement for employees

The benefits of ego-boosters:
- Increased staff confidence

- Greater loyalty and commitment to the company

- Motivated employees

The benefits of structure:
- Predictability (even in the midst of change)

- Confidence in 'the system'

- Continuity (this is not a fad)

Are you a suggestions saboteur?

Listed below are some of the tell-tale signs of the suggestions saboteur. Try not to be a 'yes man' in any of these areas.

YES	NO	
———	———	I tend to defend the company's status quo. To do otherwise would be disloyal.
———	———	I am often sceptical about change. 'If it isn't broken, it doesn't need mending.'
———	———	I remember people's failures – extremely well.
———	———	I forget people's successes – quickly.
———	———	I don't question the way things are done – they are obviously done the way they are for a reason!
———	———	I get irritated when employees ask stupid questions.

—— —— I discourage employees' contributions. If my subordinates really knew what they were talking about, they would be managers.

—— —— I sometimes take credit for ideas proposed by my subordinates.

—— —— I procrastinate. Even good employee suggestions sometimes have to wait until I can get round to them.

—— —— I don't pay enough attention to the implementation of ideas. Things often slip through the net.

—— —— I think that wanting to change the status quo is really a covert or subconscious complaint.

—— —— When employees question the way things are done, I see the situation as being one of 'us' (management) versus 'them' (employees).

—— —— I believe I know more than the employees about the working of the department. If changes were needed, I would be the one to recognise them.

—— —— I wish employees would stop trying to alter the system and just do their work!

CHAPTER 3

An Introduction to Value Management

Setting up the process

Visibility, ego-boosters and structure are the backbone of a good employee suggestion scheme. Value Management provides the muscle.

DEFINITION

Value Management is a step-by-step creative process that revolves around the word 'function'. It helps employees to identify better ways of providing necessary change.

Value Management (VM), which was created and refined at the General Electric Company in the USA, has an impressive 40-year track record. Many top companies such as Boeing, Westinghouse, Black & Decker, etc use VM to improve their product or service while cutting costs. When you use VM, you are in good company.

Companies which practise Value Management

Value Management may sound like a lot of work, but it's an investment well worth making. The following list includes just some of the companies and organisations which use Value Management:

Bell & Howell
Bendix
Black and Decker

Boeing Company
Caterpillar Tractor
Control Data
Data General
Ford Motor Company
General Electric
Hewlett-Packard
Honeywell
IBM
Ingersoll Rand
Inland Revenue
John Deere
Lockheed
NCR Corporation
Philips Industries
RCA
Stanley Tools
Union Carbide
Westinghouse

The VM ground rules

When starting up a VM suggestion scheme, it is important to establish some ground rules.

Rule 1: Don't think of VM as simple cost cutting

Concentrating on costs alone results in shoddy products, slower service and low morale. It alienates customers and drives away business. VM always considers both what you pay (costs) and what you get in return (quality). Employees should also be encouraged to submit ideas that actually *increase* costs, as long as there is an even greater increase in quality.

Rule 2: Listen via the grapevine for a negative response

Do your employees make remarks like the following?

- So-and-so isn't going to like this.

- Forget it – it's not my job!
- Perhaps one day.
- What's wrong with the way we do it now?
- What's he trying to prove?
- That's too much of a risk.
- We don't have the money to waste on that.
- Why bother?

If so, your scheme isn't doing its job. It hasn't answered the fundamental question: 'What's in it for me?'

Rule 3: Give employees directions rather than directives

Steer employees towards successful suggestions. Encourage them to look at the parts of their job that are:

- More complicated than necessary
- Frustrating (things are often frustrating because they are poorly designed)
- Possible to change and improve
- Not standard, or unique to your company (do your competitors operate differently because they know something you don't?)

Teach employees to ask the crucial tests of value:

- Does this product/component/task add value?
- Is it worth what it costs (£1-worth of use for £1 in costs)?
- Are all its features required?
- Can anything else do the same job?
- Are other companies paying less for the item? Could we?

- Can it be made or completed in a less expensive way?
- Are we using the right 'tools' (technology, parts, training)?

Rule 4: Give your employees more authority

Give your employees the basic tools of authority:

- Access to information
- The right to challenge old ideas
- The freedom to ask 'stupid' questions (there are no stupid questions, only stupid mistakes)
- Open lines of communication

The six tasks of Value Management

Value Management involves six separate and important tasks (the same steps apply to any VM target: services, systems, processes, procedures):

Task 1: Gather information
Collect the information needed to understand and analyse the product.

Task 2: Identify functions
Define the product: not what it *is*, but what it *does*. (This step is what separates VM from all other analytical techniques. Other approaches look for incremental improvements; VM's functional bias allows employees to address more basic – and much more profitable – issues.)

Task 3: Generate ideas
Identify new ways of providing the required functions.

Task 4: Consolidate ideas
Analyse the ideas and direct the best ones into a few possible new products.

Task 5: Evaluate alternatives
Look for the combination of ideas that will provide all the required functions at the lowest cost.

Task 6: Recommend the idea
Submit the best idea to the suggestions committee for review and action.

The tasks set in the next chapter should be passed on to employees. They will give employees a better idea of what VM is all about and help to provide a framework for profitable employee suggestions.

CHAPTER 4
The VM Tasks

Task 1: Gather information

> *Goal*: To gather all the information needed to understand – and eventually analyse – the product in question.

Write a description of the product. Imagine you're describing it to someone who has never seen it – or anything like it – before. What would he or she need to know?

Answer such questions as: What is the product? What does it consist of? How does it work? What does it do? Does it do what it is supposed to do? What kind of track record does it have? What does it do well? Where does it fall short? What do people like or dislike about the product? What does it cost to produce (labour, materials, overheads)?

The amount of detail required will depend on the product. Add as many pages as you need.

DESCRIPTION

_____

_____

_____

_____

_____

_____

_____

_____

_____

_____

_____

Task 2: Identify functions

> *Goal*: To define the product completely in terms of what it does and what it must do.

Fill in the 'Product Functions' chart on page 32, using the following guidelines:

Step 1: Describe the product through its functions
List everything the product does using only two words per function, a noun and a verb. For example, when used by a person, a pen *draws lines, writes letters, holds ink, prevents leaks*, and so on. If you can't describe a function in two words, break it up into sub-functions. For example, the retractable tip function of a ballpoint pen could be described as 'tip can be retracted when not in use' – but that takes too many words. Break it down into two functions: *retracts tip, extends tip*.

Step 2: Sort the functions into order of priority
Every product has one primary function (what it must do) and numerous secondary functions (extras). Rank the functions that you've listed in order of importance: 1 for the primary function, 2 for the most important secondary function, and so on.

Step 3: Categorise the functions
There are two types of functions: 'work' functions and 'selling' functions. Work functions are what make the product work: they are described by concrete verbs and nouns (for example, *draws lines*). Selling functions are what make the product sale-able and are described by abstract verbs and nouns (for example, *increases prestige*). Go through your list of functions and mark the work functions with W and the selling functions with S.

PRODUCT FUNCTIONS

Step 1: Function		Step 2: Priority	Step 3: Category
Verb	*Noun*	*Rank*	*Work or Selling*

A functional example

Functional analysis is more difficult than it sounds. It is essential to get down to basics. Consider the following example:

The product: a gold-plated pen with corporate logo.

Step 1: Describe the product through its functions
What does this pen do? What functions does it provide?

> It draws lines, writes letters, holds ink, prevents leaks, retracts tip, extends tip, prevents evaporation, increases prestige, provides advertising.

Step 2: Sort the functions into order of priority
What is the primary thing that the pen must do?

> That depends. If the pen is meant to be used regularly, its primary function is *draws lines* or *writes letters*. If it was designed strictly as an expensive advertisement for the company, its primary function is *increases prestige*. Let's assume that the pen will be used regularly for writing.

Step 3: Categorise the functions
What must the pen do in order to work?

> It must draw lines, write letters, hold ink, prevent leaks, retract tip, extend tip, prevent evaporation.

What must the pen do in order to sell?

> It must increase prestige, provide advertising.

The 'Product Functions' chart for the gold-plated pen with corporate logo (page 32) would look something like this:

PRODUCT FUNCTIONS

Step 1: Function		Step 2: Priority	Step 3: Category
Verb	*Noun*	*Rank*	*Work or Selling*
draws	lines	1	W
writes	letters	1	W
holds	ink	2	W

Step 1: Function		Step 2: Priority	Step 3: Category
Verb	*Noun*	*Rank*	*Work or Selling*
prevents	leaks	3	W
extends	tip	5	W
retracts	tip	6	W
prevents	evaporation	4	W
increases	prestige	8	S
provides	advertising	7	S

Functional mistakes

Identifying these functional mistakes can lead to significant savings:

- *Unnecessary work functions*
  Work functions that don't increase the product's usefulness are unnecessary functions. Unnecessary functions waste money.

  Example: the pen may conduct electricity, but that isn't important to penmanship. If the company is paying more for this work function, it is wasting money.

- *Unnecessary selling functions*
  Selling functions that don't affect the product's saleability are also unnecessary functions that waste money.

  Example: the pen is gold-plated to increase prestige. However, unseen gold-plating on the inside would be a waste of money.

- *Money-wasting functions*
  Functions that cost more than they are worth waste money.

  Example: salespeople could be given solid gold pens with the company logo. Such pens would certainly be prestigious, but the cost would be astronomical.

Task 3: Generate ideas

Goal: To identify new ways of providing the required functions.

Task 3 aims to generate a long list of different ways of providing the product's necessary functions.

This is easier than it sounds because the immediate goal is quantity, not quality, of ideas. *Task 3* will set the creative mechanism in motion, without allowing the restrictions of premature judgements, ridicule or censorship to get in the way. Ideas should be allowed to run the gamut from sensational to plain stupid.

After working through the general questions on pages 35–7, fill in the remaining sections of *Task 3* (pages 38–43) for each function. Write down anything that comes to mind and go straight on. Don't stop to think! You will end up with a comprehensive list of alternatives.

Getting started

Asking these general questions is a good way to get the creative process working.

Product particulars

- What can be learned from analysing what the product *isn't*?

_____

_____

_____

- What are the benefits and advantages of this product?

_____

_____

_____

- What are the drawbacks or disadvantages of this product?

_____

_____

_____

- Can one component be modified to provide additional functions?

_____

_____

_____

- Can one function be split among several components?

_____

_____

_____

Personal preferences

- If I were designing this product from scratch, is this how I would provide the necessary functions? What would I have done instead?

_____

_____

_____

- What don't I like about the product? Is anything unsatisfactory?

_____

_____

_____

Competitive questions

- How do our competitors provide similar functions?

_____

_____

_____

• Do our competitors provide better functions (less expensive, more reliable, more attractive)?

_____

_____

_____

• How do we and our products differ from the competition?

_____

_____

_____

• What is better, or worse, about competitors' products?

_____

_____

_____

• What positive comments do customers make about competitors' products?

_____

_____

_____

• Why do we lose customers to the competition?

_____

_____

_____

37

The functional basics

> *Function No:*

- Is this function necessary? Could it be eliminated?

_____

_____

- How important is it?

_____

_____

- Is there a different or better way of providing it? For example?

_____

_____

_____

- Would adding this function give the product more value?

_____

_____

- Would increasing this function give the product more value?

_____

- Would decreasing this function give the product more value?

_____

- Would subtracting this function give the product more value?

_____

Function No:

What changes might improve the product? It might be possible to:

Make it longer _____

Make it shorter _____

Make it bigger _____

Make it smaller _____

Make it stronger _____

Make it weaker _____

Make it thicker _____

Make it thinner _____

Make it more expensive (designer)_____

Make it cheaper _____

Make it hot _____

Make it cold _____

Make it one-piece _____

Make it multi-piece _____

Make it disposable _____

Make it reusable _____

Make it centralised _____

Make it decentralised _____

Make it faster _____

Make it slower _____

Make it simpler _____

Make it more complex_____

It might be possible to:

Make it softer _____

Make it harder _____

Make it rough _____

Make it smooth _____

Change its shape _____

Change its direction _____

Change its orientation _____

Change its positioning _____

Merge its pieces _____

Converge its pieces _____

Stratify its pieces _____

Combine its pieces _____

Redefine its character _____

Substitute parts _____

Interchange parts _____

Upgrade parts _____

Replace parts _____

Standardise parts _____

Stabilise parts _____

Reverse something _____

Improve resilience _____

Use colour _____

Change its form _____

Incorporate separate functions into the basic unit_____

Preform components _____

Conform _____

Creativity by numbers

The rule of 15
Pick one function from the chart on page 32. Write down 15 different ways (even impractical ones!) of providing that function.

Example: for the function *connects papers*, ideas might include staples, paper clips, sewing, chewing gum, welding torch, nuclear fusion.

Function No:

Ways of providing this function:

1. _____

2. _____

3. _____

4. _____

5. _____

6. _____

7. _____

8. _____

9. _____

10. _____

11. _____

12. _____

13. _____

14. _____

15. _____

The rule of 26

Take one function. Write down 26 ways of providing that function, one for each letter of the alphabet (don't worry if you miss a few letters, such as x, y or z). Look in the dictionary for inspiration (for example: A – abolish, absorb, accelerate, accent, etc).

Function No:

Ways of providing this function:

A	
B	
C	
D	
E	
F	
G	
H	
I	
J	
K	
L	
M	
N	
O	
P	
Q	
R	
S	
T	
U	
V	
W	
X	
Y	
Z	

Concentrate on the verb for work functions

Forget the function's noun and concentrate only on the verb. Why? A two-word function like *attach tag* may generate only three ideas (tie, staple, clamp); an unrestricted verb, *attach*, will generate many more (freeze, Velcro, graft, suction . . .).

Note: This technique only works on work functions.

Verb: _____

Ways of providing this function:

1. _____
2. _____
3. _____
4. _____
5. _____
6. _____
7. _____
8. _____
9. _____
10. _____
11. _____
12. _____
13. _____
14. _____
15. _____

Task 4: Consolidate ideas

Goal: To direct our creative ideas into a few workable alternatives.

Step 1: Analyse the ideas

This is 'judgement day.' The ideas generated during *Task 3* need to be analysed and judged. Some are simply impractical. Those that could be practical need to be assessed. Each idea has its own set of advantages and disadvantages and it is important to identify these pros and cons.

The first time round, use a pencil – this form will probably be revised again and again . . .

Function No:

Creative ideas to provide this function	Advantages	Disadvantages	Costs*

*Costs include labour, overheads, raw materials, components, tools and equipment. Don't be overwhelmed. For simple projects, relative costs or common sense are enough (for example, if it takes twice as long to do it this way, the labour costs will be double.)

These pros and cons are not fixed. Review and amend them with the following questions in mind.

- Can the advantages or impact of this idea be strengthened? How?

_____

_____

_____

- Can the disadvantages be lessened? How?

_____

_____

_____

- Can this idea be combined with others to give more advantages or fewer disadvantages? How?

_____

_____

_____

Step 2: Combine the ideas

The creative ideas for the separate functions need to be brought together. The following form makes this easy.

Product:

FUNCTION 1	
1. Idea that best provides function 1 at the lowest cost	
FUNCTION 2	
2. Idea that best provides function 2 at the lowest cost and combines best with idea 1	

FUNCTION 3	
3. Idea that best provides function 3 at the lowest cost and combines best with ideas 1 and 2	
FUNCTION 4	
4. Idea that best provides function 4 at the lowest cost and combines best with idea 1, 2 and 3	

It will be necessary to compromise. For example, cost concerns become more and more important as the function becomes less important – you want to pay as little as possible for unimportant functions. No one idea will fulfil a function perfectly, fit in with other ideas, and have the lowest cost – but one will probably come closer than any of the others. The key question is: Which idea offers the best value?

Repeat this process using the second best idea for function 1, then the third best idea. In this way you will come up with several potential products. These can then be compared and contrasted.

Step 3: Compare and contrast

Use the following questions to compare and contrast the product alternatives:

- What are the advantages of each alternative?

Alternative 1 _____

Alternative 2 _____

Alternative 3 _____

- What are the disadvantages?

Alternative 1 _____

Alternative 2 _____

Alternative 3 _____

• Do the advantages outweigh the disadvantages?

Alternative 1 _____

Alternative 2 _____

Alternative 3 _____

• What tradeoffs are involved?

Alternative 1 _____

Alternative 2 _____

Alternative 3 _____

• Can disadvantages be turned into solvable problems or advantages?

Alternative 1 _____

Alternative 2 _____

Alternative 3 _____

• Do the advantages of any alternative justify making a change to the existing product?

_____

_____

_____

• Which alternative is the best? For what reasons – and by how much of a margin?

Best _____

Second best _____

Third best _____

• In what way are the alternatives similar?

_____

_____

_____

- How do the alternatives differ?

_____

_____

_____

- Can alternatives be combined or adjusted to create a better option?

_____

_____

_____

Task 5: Evaluate alternatives

> _Goal_: To gather all the information necessary to analyse – and judge – the alternative products.

Task 5 is essentially an insurance policy. It ensures that the alternative recommended will offer the best value – that it provides all the functions with high quality at a low cost.

Ask these four questions about each alternative:

1. Should standard components be used?

   Rationale: Standard components tend to have a lower cost, better reputation, greater reliability and be more readily available than those that are made to order.

2. Would a made-to-order component offer the best value?

   Rationale: New technology or procedures may make special orders the best option.

3. What do the experts think?

   Rationale: Check with peers, managers, suppliers, customers, professional associations, trade journals, academics and anyone else you can think of for feedback. They may have a different perspective, and may ask valid questions that you haven't thought of.

4. Has the final idea had time to settle?

   Rationale: Waiting a week before submitting any idea will allow time for any last-minute inspirations.

Task 6: Recommend the idea

> *Goal*: To present the idea to the suggestions committee in such a way that it will be accepted and implemented.

In some respects, *Task 6* is more important than any of its counterparts. Unless the idea is accepted and implemented, the first five tasks were of little value.

Here are some tips for dealing with suggestions committees:

- Make yourself familiar with the committee members. Who are they? What do they like? What motivates them (is it primarily cost or quality)? Consider showing them background material (the VM forms).

- Always include cost information. Overestimate costs and underestimate savings. That way, any surprises will be good surprises.

- Give plenty of facts and few 'guesstimates'. Committee members can't dismiss relevant, verifiable, objective facts.

- Include 'before and after' comparisons (costs, problems, opportunities, improvements) so that committee members will understand the benefits of a suggestion.

- Show the how and why of any conclusions.

- Stress the benefits of the idea. What will the company gain by implementing it?

- Find a devil's advocate who is prepared to be critical of the idea. If there's a serious wrinkle in the fabric of an idea the time to iron it out is before – not during – presentation to the committee.

- If appropriate, suggest a schedule or strategy for implementation.

CHAPTER 5
Case Study

The following is a real-life case study. It demonstrates how a successful employee suggestion scheme, teamed with viable VM, can yield unheard-of benefits. In this case, productivity on a single business form increased by 800 per cent, while error rates dropped from 68 per cent to 2 per cent. Morale and departmental turnover improved, and costs (recruitment, training, production, returns, corrections, postage, materials) plummeted.

It provides a lesson on how employee suggestion and VM schemes can lessen common management problems:

- They turn a problem situation into an opportunity.

- They facilitate the delegation of important tasks. Here the manager isn't just delegating a task, he or she is passing on the means to accomplish it.

- They allow managers to enhance their training efforts. Suggestion schemes and VM guidelines are used again and again by motivated employees.

- They enhance teamwork (particularly between managers and employees). There is no 'us-versus-them', 'employees-versus-management' mentality. The prevailing perspective becomes 'us versus it': employees *and* managers versus the problem.

- They help managers to transcend 'management' and ascend to 'leadership'.

The WC105 problem

'Great minds think alike', thought George when he heard complaints about form WC105 coming from the typing pool. Form WC105 had a bad reputation with typists. It was frustrating, difficult to type and irritating to work with. Top typists considered themselves lucky to type 6 words per minute on WC105. The departmental average on other forms was 52 words per minute. No wonder it was the form everybody loved to hate.

George's perspective was different, but no less negative. This form had the lowest productivity level of any in the company (only 10 words took 1 minute 39 seconds to type!). It created low morale and low quality standards (it had an incredible 68 per cent error rate), high turnover and high costs. Clearly, something had to be done. George decided to help Marion, an experienced and innovative member of staff, to solve the problem by using VM.

Write what you think George should do in the space provided below. Then compare your answer with that of the author on page 53.

_____

_____

_____

_____

_____

_____

_____

_____

_____

_____

George's plan of action

The following is what George decided to do to help Marion to apply VM techniques to the problem.

- *Help Marion to spot the potential for improvement*
  Form WC105 is frustrating to type because it is poorly designed. That makes it an excellent candidate for the suggestion scheme.

- *Stress the benefits*
  What benefits will Marion gain by participating in the suggestion scheme? (Personal recognition, improved productivity, less stressful work, possibly financial compensation . . .)

- *Encourage Marion to use the VM process*
  VM won't just show Marion where to start – it will tell her where to go. VM is her most direct route to the best option.

- *Provide the necessary support*
  Give Marion the resources she needs to analyse the form fully (VM and general information, undisturbed periods, access to other departments). Help her to identify potential pitfalls (both practical and political). Be there with moral and managerial support (including feedback, encouragement and praise).

In short, facilitate, rather than hinder, Marion's efforts. That's what management – and Value Management – is all about.

A detailed solution

Task 1: Gather information
George's initial *Task 1* actions are as follows:

- Give Marion the first VM form (on page 30.) Discuss how to write a description and provide examples.

- Acknowledge the problems with form WC105. Stress Marion's right to ask any questions she sees fit.

- Answer any questions Marion might have about the suggestion scheme or the VM process (of which she will have little, if any, knowledge). Suggest that she takes each step as it comes rather than trying to get one step ahead.

Here is a summary of Marion's findings:

WC105 is a form used on 5 per cent of all new insurance policies. It consists of two similar pieces of paper (A and B). These are sheets of white A5 paper, printed on the front and back. They look identical; the only difference is that A is printed on NCR (No Carbon Required) paper. A and B are attached at the top in such a way that they can be pulled apart. Copy A is for our use, copy B is for the clients. A copy of the form is attached.

Each sheet contains seven blocks of information. The fronts contain an address block and three sections of client data. The backs contain three more client sections.

We type the address block. Some or all of the six client sections must be completed. We type Xs in front of those. We send the form to the client, who completes it. He or she separates the two sheets, keeps the second sheet for a record and sends us back the top copy.

The most we ever type is a client's name and address and six Xs, yet the form takes an average of 1 minute 39 seconds to complete. This works out at an average typing speed of 6 words per minute. On our other departmental forms the average speed is 52 words per minute.

Productivity is very low on form WC105 because completing it requires up to 26 steps:

Step 1	Insert the front of the form.
Step 2	Align the paper.
Step 3	Type the client's name and address.
Step 4	Realign the paper
Step 5	Type the first X.
Step 6	Realign the paper.
Step 7	Type the second X.
Step 8	Realign the paper.

Step 9   Type the third X.
Step 10   Remove the paper.

Thanks to NCR paper, steps 1–10 complete the fronts of sheets A and B. However, NCR paper doesn't work both ways. The backs of sheets A and B must be completed separately, while the two sheets remain attached at the top.

Step 11   Insert the back of sheet B.
Step 12   Align the paper.
Step 13   Type the fourth X.
Step 14   Realign the paper.
Step 15   Type the fifth X.
Step 16   Realign the paper.
Step 17   Type the sixth X.
Step 18   Remove the paper.

Now comes the hardest part:

Steps 19–26 Repeat steps 11–18 for the back of sheet A.

Form WC105 is universally disliked. Clients find it difficult to fill in properly and it often comes back incomplete. (For example, the client only fills in the back of sheet B, then sends us back sheet A – with the back not completed!) When this happens, we have to type another WC105 and resubmit it to the client, hoping he or she will fill it in correctly the second time.

George's follow-up *Task 1* actions are:

- Discuss the description with Marion. Provide feedback or insight by means of questions: Is there anything else you need to know? Aren't there rather a lot of repetitive steps? Isn't there an awful lot of effort for so little typing?

- Provide additional encouragement. Marion has five more steps to go.

Task 2: Identify functions
George's initial *Task 2* actions are as follows:

- Give Marion the second VM form (the 'Product Functions'

chart on pages 33–4.) Discuss how it works and provide examples, if possible from a similar project.

- Stress the importance of taking VM one step at a time. This step can seem so simplistic that it is often hurried through. Explain to Marion that it's this particular step that makes the process so successful, so it's worth spending some time on it.

- Complete the *Task 2* form himself. Why? Spotting all the necessary product functions can be tricky, particularly the first time. By compiling his own list of functions, George can compare his conclusions with Marion's. If necessary, he can suggest that she considers additional functions – not to second-guess Marion, but to provide a back-up. It's essential to cover all functions; missing some of them would cripple the VM's effectiveness and hinder Marion's efforts.

Here is a summary of Marion's findings:

Form WC105 has five functions:

> to collect information, instruct client, make copies, separate copies, categorise information.

The ranking in order of priority is as follows:

> Priority 1: Collect information
> Priority 2: Categorise information
> Priority 3: Instruct client
> Priority 4: Make copies
> Priority 5: Separate copies

Work or selling functions:

> All are work functions

George's follow-up *Task 2* actions are:

- Use feedback to help Marion to question the status quo. For example:

Does WC105's primary function – *collect information* –

require its own form? (Could this data be collected on the original insurance application, for example ?)

Is enough emphasis put on providing the primary function? (Obviously not, when there is a 68 per cent error rate!)

Is it necessary to *categorise information*? Directing clients to categories requires a lot of effort. Could clients simply be asked to complete all appropriate questions?

Steps 4–26 fulfill the *instruct client* function, by telling the client which sections to complete. Could we rearrange the instructions to the client so that 88 per cent of our efforts are not wasted on secondary concerns?

Are the two 'copy' functions necessary (*make copies* and *separate copies*)? The copies are what complicate this form. Would it be possible for clients to take their own photocopies?

- Encourage Marion not just to think, but to 'think big'!

Task 3: Generate ideas
George's initial *Task 3* actions are:

- Give Marion the appropriate VM forms (see pages 35–43). Discuss how these forms work and provide examples.

- Provide the necessary backup. *Task 3* can be long and frustrating. Follow Marion's progress closely. Provide encouragement and subtle prompting. Assist with research and contacts.

Here is a summary of Marion's creative ideas:

Function 1: *Collect information*
In this the best way to collect information? Could we substitute another method: use the phone; ask agents to submit the data when appropriate (either through an agent-based form or through a regular memo); add these questions to other forms (the original application form, other follow-up WC forms); send all clients a generic WC105 form and ask them to fill out any relevant sections; adopt a computer-generated form that includes only the sections necessary for that particular client?

Are we collecting information efficiently and effectively? Could we delete redundant or unnecessary data?; ask for more data (for example, three years' wage records rather than just the most recent quarter's)?; require a better class of data (for example, audited rather than informal accounts)?; request comments (for example, if the answer is not positive, does the client have an explanation)?; use 'exception' reporting (since the form only applies to 5 per cent of all clients, and only 5 per cent of returned forms will require further action, couldn't we ask clients to complete certain sections only if certain conditions exist)?

Is this the best format for collecting information? Could we make this a one-sided form by using longer or wider paper, narrower margins, smaller type, less copy?; use carbon paper instead of NCR paper? (turning carbon paper over is faster than retyping a page); use double-sided carbon paper? (strategically placed 'holes' in the carbon paper would allow typists to type the front of both pages simultaneously then turn the form over and type the backs simultaneously).

Function 2: *Categorise information*
Could we eliminate sections and simply ask clients to complete the relevant questions?; make each section a separate piece of paper and insert pages rather than type instructions (a process already used on endorsement sheets)?; align all columns vertically to eliminate realignments?; use colour-coded sections for easy reference?; use fewer categories?; name the categories, rather than simply identifying them with Xs?

Function 3: *Instruct client*
Could we improve communications by using bigger print, clearer wording, coloured type?; type all instructions in one place, replacing Xs with letters referring to the sections ('Complete sections A and E')?; write Xs by hand to eliminate typing?

Functions 4 and 5: *Make copies and separate copies*
Could we eliminate the copy function entirely and suggest

that clients make their own photocopies? (With the existing WC105, sheet B is not a true copy of sheet A, since the back pages are actually typed separately.) Could we get clients to complete a one-page WC105 form, then send it back to them when we have finished with it (keeping a photocopy for our files, if desired)?

George's follow-up *Task 3* actions are:

- Provide feedback without making negative judgements.

- Encourage Marion to get ideas from other sources (peers, other departments, designers, managers, agents, clients, printers).

Task 4: Consolidate ideas
George's initial *Task 4* actions:

- Give Marion the appropriate VM forms (on pages 44–8). Discuss how they work and provide examples.

- Remind Marion that the alternatives she comes up with can be quite different from the current process. Encourage major overhauls. Major overhauls bring major improvements.

- Offer to help with feedback or refinements whenever necessary.

Here is a summary of Marion's alternatives:

Alternative 1
Eliminate form WC105. Ask agents to add the information to an insurance application whenever necessary. This could be done via a new form WC105 or a regular memo.

Alternative 2
Send out a revised generic WC105 form to all new policy-holders. Ask them to complete any applicable questions.

Alternative 3

Redesign the form to fit on to one side of a larger sheet of paper. Print all instructions in one area. Specify which lettered sections the client should complete ('Please complete sections A and E'). Eliminate sheet B; add a sentence to the instructions suggesting that the client will only be sent a copy if he specifically requests it.

The new form's instructions would look something like those shown below.

Client's name and address: [without the lines, which used to require paper alignment]

Please complete section(s):   and return the completed form to this office. A copy will only be sent if specifically requested.

Completing this form would require only six steps, instead of the current form's 26 steps.

Step 1   Insert the form.
Step 2   Align the paper.
Step 3   Type the client's name and address.
Step 4   Go to the space after the instruction 'Please complete section(s)'.
Step 5   Type the letters for the sections to be filled in (A, B, C, D, E, and/or F).
Step 6   Remove the paper.

Alternative 4

Same as alternative 3, except that a second page (a coloured client copy) is attached. The top sheet would be a tear-off NCR sheet. Instruct the client to remove and keep the coloured sheet.

George's follow-up *Task 4* actions:

- Help Marion to refine her alternatives. Add additional perspective and guidance regarding office politics, acceptability, costs.

- Offer an assessment (positive perspective) without being over-critical (negative perspective).

Task 5: Evaluate alternatives
George's initial *Task 5* actions are:

- Encourage Marion to reconsider her alternatives.
- Facilitate the feedback process. Give help in soliciting ideas and cushion any harsh criticisms. Help to interpret advice. Propose written feedback for possible submission to the suggestions committee.

These are Marion's findings:

Standardised or made-to-order materials were not major factors in this study. However, expert feedback (from peers, manager, agents, clients) played a crucial role. For example:

Alternative 1, getting agents to collect this information, when appropriate, was judged politically impractical. The company was trying desperately to improve the agents' productivity so any increase in their workload was not a good idea.

Alternative 2, developing a generic form and getting clients to answer any applicable questions, was more popular with the experts. But there was one drawback: would policyholders always know which questions were applicable? Alternative 2 could create more problems than it solved.

Alternative 3, designing a larger, one-page form was very popular. Twenty production steps were eliminated. So was the copy, which turned out to be quite unnecessary. Marion learned that 82 per cent of all clients did not keep a copy of the form. Those who did often made a photocopy of the original form. Alternative 3 maximised the necessary functions and didn't waste time or money on providing peripherals.

Alternative 4, adding a client copy to Alternative 3, was seen as functionally acceptable, but not as efficient as Alternative 3. The cost of providing a tear-off copy was seen as unnecessary.

Miriam decided to submit Alternative 3 to the suggestion committee.

George's follow-up *Task 5* actions are:

• Review Marion's information and conclusion. Ask questions and clarify.

• Note the quality of feedback received from the experts. George may wish to consult them again for future projects.

Task 6: Recommend the idea
George's initial *Task 6* actions are:

• Discuss the presentation to the suggestions committee with Marion. Answer any questions and allay any fears.

• Help Marion to prepare her presentation. Act as a practice 'audience.'

• Make sure that Marion has all the material and equipment she needs to make a formal presentation of her idea.

• Help Marion to secure a champion for her idea on the suggestions committee.

Marion goes about presenting her idea as follows:

She gets a mock-up of the proposed Alternative 3 form which she submits to the suggestions committee, along with her completed suggestion form and back-up material (all the VM forms she has filled in).

On the day of the presentation, she and George arrive at the suggestions committee meeting with a typewriter, a pending

WC file, a WC105 form, an Alternative 3 form, and the back-up material. Marion's supporter on the committee has already discussed her idea with the other members and given his own positive recommendation.

Using information from the pending WC file, Marion completes a WC105 form. Time taken: 1 minute 45 seconds. Using the same WC file, she completes an Alternative 3 form in 12 seconds. She explains how her alternative reduces typing errors and client errors. Clearly, it is worth pursuing.

She offers to answer any questions from the suggestions committee, but there are none. In fact, there is no opposition to her well-presented, well-documented alternative. The suggestion is unanimously accepted and implemented immediately.

George's follow-up *Task 6* action:

- Celebrate. Marion's success is his success too.

Task 7:
You are probably wondering what this is, as Value Management requires only six tasks. *Task 7* has nothing to do with Value Management and everything to do with just plain management. It is the checklist that George uses to ensure that this one success fertilises many future suggestions, both from Marion and from the other typists.

**Tick box
when
completed**

☐ Congratulate Marion publicly and privately.

☐ Buy cakes for the entire department!

☐ Write the managing director a letter outlining Marion's success.

☐ Draft a congratulatory letter for the managing director to sign and send to Marion.

☐ Get the approval form from the suggestions committee framed for Marion. Ask the maintenance department to put it up near her desk.

☐ Send Marion a letter of thanks and admiration on personal stationery.

☐ Ask Marion to demonstrate and explain the form to the other typists. Let her be 'queen for a day.'

☐ Talk to Marion about her financial reward (at this company, employees receive 5 per cent of all savings resulting from an adopted suggestion, for a period of two years and up to a maximum of £10,000 – a level that Marion's idea reaches easily).

☐ Get a copy of the suggestions committee's comments – both for Marion's benefit and for yours. What impresses them? What are they looking for? What part of the idea presentation had the most impact?

☐ Send a written 'thank you' to all the experts who provided feedback. Their help can be crucial in developing future ideas.

☐ Devote a week on the external notice-board to Marion and her idea.

☐ Have Marion's success announced over the office loudspeaker.

☐ Inform everyone involved about the outcome of the presentation. Everyone who played a part in creating or developing the idea is part of the success story.

☐ Post Marion's suggestion and her picture on the staff noticeboard.

☐ Get congratulatory leaflets designed and printed. Distribute them widely – to colleagues in Marion's department, people she works with in other departments, insurance agents in her area . . .

☐ Put Marion's name forward for the free weekend and/or 'employee of the month award'.

☐ Start the next departmental meeting by acknowledging Marion and her idea.

☐ Send a 'thank you' card round the department and get everybody to sign it.

☐ Publicise Marion's idea to various professionals in the company and encourage them to refer to it in speeches, memos, training schemes, the company newsletter, quarterly report, company advertising.

☐ Stick Marion's picture and a write-up of her idea in the company scrapbook.

☐ Send a press release about Marion's success to the local newspaper, the agent's newsletter, insurance trade journals, etc.

☐ Send a copy of Marion's idea to the department that designed the form in the first place. Maybe they can learn something!

☐ Write a note for Marion's records documenting her success.

☐ Post Marion's suggestion and her picture in reception.

☐ Ask Marion and the other typists if there is anything else they would like to see changed. If there is, consider applying the Value Management procedure.

CHAPTER 6
Conclusion

We began by talking about return on investment, and how it was rarely of importance to top managers in the long run.

It is clear that employee suggestion schemes and Value Management are an entirely different story. With the help of these procedures, a manager can reduce costs while improving product or service quality, productivity, morale, turnover, reliability, creativity, teamwork and leadership.

The suggestion/VM combination is one of the few partnerships in business that is truly a 'winners all' situation. The only losers are those who don't embark on the scheme.

Suggestion schemes in a nutshell

Good employee suggestion schemes are not just meaningless. They require a solid structure: the scheme must have easy access; employees should know what to expect and should get what they expect; the scheme should be designed for ease of use and the minimum of tension. In short, this profit-building scheme should be given the same businesslike attention as other areas of profit.

Visibility is also critical to a successful scheme. Publicity pays; promote the suggestion scheme and the employees who participate in it – everybody wants their moment in the spotlight. By highlighting successful employee innovations, you not only let employees shine – you shine by reflected glory.

The ego-boosters built into a successful suggestion scheme are the building blocks for future success. These 'pats on the back' increase employee confidence and creativity. Employees with a higher level of self-esteem turn in a higher number of profitable ideas.

Strong employee suggestion schemes are a means to an important end. Companies that regard their suggestion schemes as non-essential will not get the best results.

Value Management: a résumé

Value Management is a set of techniques that help employees to identify creative ways of providing product or service functions. The steps are clear and concise:

1. Gather the information needed to analyse the product.

2. Define the product in terms of what it does and what it must do.

3. Identify new ways of providing these functions.

4. Direct these ideas into a few workable alternatives.

5. Evaluate the proposed alternatives.

6. Recommend the best alternative.

However, the steps that management needs to take to make the suggestion work are less clear. It's important that you create a positive attitude. You must guide employees through the value process without making them feel restricted or pampered. Remember, you can give employees the tools to think, but they have to do the thinking.

Further Reading from Kogan Page

Creative Thinking in Business, Carol Kinsey Goman
Don't Do. Delegate!, J M Jenks and J M Kelly
The First Time Manager, M J Morris
How To Be an Even Better Manager, Michael Armstrong
How to Develop a Positive Attitude, Elwood N Chapman
How to Motivate People, Twyla Dell
Improving Relations at Work, Elwood N Chapman
Project Management: From Idea to Implementation, Marion E
   Haynes
Team Building, Robert B Maddux